For my dear ████
Marge and ████ Kein
with love and appreciation

Charlotte Phyfer
August, 1981

And now to our dear
daughter with love
█ ███ giving ████ ███ ████ of
Mississippi.

Dad. Mother
Feb. 11, 1997

BAYOU AUTUMN

Poetry by
Charlotte Phyfer

DORRANCE & COMPANY, INCORPORATED
CRICKET TERRACE CENTER • ARDMORE, PENNSYLVANIA 19003
Publishers Since 1920

ACKNOWLEDGMENT

Some of the poems included in this volume appeared in *Mississippi Verse*, edited by Alice James (Chapel Hill: Univ. of North Carolina Press, 1934), and are included with the permission of the publisher.

The following poems first appeared in the *Christian Science Monitor:* "New Brooms," "Yesterday," "Teton Sunrise," "Streets of Cintra—Portugal," "Japanese Fan," "Simplicity," "Minstrelsy," "Little Boats of Jerba," "September Roadways," "Reverie," and "November Twilight."

To my dear friend
Frances
in appreciation of
her unfailing
encouragement

CONTENTS

BAYOU AUTUMN

The bayou sings in autumn
When spotted bass are running
And the willow's golden tresses
Are hanging out for sunning;
My clumsy pirogue dances
As my paddle dips and swings,
Autumn on the bayou—
What happy days it brings!

SOUTHERN SEPTEMBER

September brings to southern woods
And sleepy roadside places,
Wild asters of the palest blue,
The ragweed's simple graces.
Little breezes echo
The ringdove's plaintive cries;
The fields burn bright with goldenrod
And tawny butterflies.
Remembering stars above the river
On a warm September night,
September seems in southern woods
A season of delight.

RETICENCE

It may be I shall tell you by and by
How you fill all my dreams by night and day,
How lonely is my heart with you away.
I cannot tell you now, I know not why.
There may be words for what I long to tell,
How all of happiness for me now lies
Within your hand—my peace within your eyes;
How I have loved but you both long and well.
Words, and to spare, to speak of things apart—
Of ferns, and streams, and notes of singing birds,
Of rain in summer; yet I have no words
To tell you what I find within my heart.
And, lacking words for what I long to say,
I pray that you may know some other way.

SEPTEMBER ROADWAYS

Woodside roadways in September
Fill my heart with glee!
Ageratum, goldenrod,
Black-eyed Susans dance and nod.
Woodside roadways, in September,
Bring a song to me!

INDIAN SUMMER

When with the cycle of the years
Each blue October comes again,
I shall see—perhaps through tears—
This dusty stretch of country lane.
I shall hear the ring-dove's cries,
Watch russet leaves that drift and fall,
See goldenrod, bright butterflies,
The pines that stand serene and tall.
And I shall see your shining face
And spread my hands before its glow
To warm my heart a little space
Before the winds of winter blow.

BAYOU SUNSETS

The wind blows through the willows
At the water's edge,
And slender are the shadows
That stretch from tree and hedge;
The piping chimney-swallows
Fly swift on whirring wings,
Sunsets on the bayou
Are made of lovely things!

OCTOBER MORNING

It seems as if October
Was made for folks like me!
The leaves are red and yellow
On every sweet-gum tree;
Meadowlarks are singing,
From tree to hedge they dart.
October mornings make me feel
So cheerful in my heart!

OCTOBER

October is a blue month,
These things abide for proof:
Michaelmas daisies in the sun,
Blue-purple haze when day is done,
Blue wood-smoke spiraling
Upward from a roof.

NOVEMBER TWILIGHT

Peace fills my heart at twilight
On November days—
When distant hills stand shrouded
In dusky haze,
And violet are the shadows
That slip across the plain.
And little breezes carry scents
Of pine trees after rain.

TAMBOURINE

The summer wind is a minstrel
With a lute of forest trees,
The winter wind is a mariner
With songs of the seven seas;
Wind is a weaver in rainy spring
With threads of silver sheen,
But the autumn wind is a gypsy
With a rattling tambourine!

THREE SONGS

Three songs are there
From others set apart:
The paean of praise
From a grateful heart,
Bird-song in winter
At the close of day,
And sound of singing water
From far away.

DISCOVERY

Still lingers beauty in the woods
On a winter's day:
Water oaks beside a stream
And careless squirrels at play,
Leaves that crackle underfoot,
Moss that trails from trees;
Surely summer never brought
Treasures such as these!
April rains bring daffodils,
The hawthorn buds in May,
Yet beauty lingers in the woods
On a winter's day.

PREFERENCE

Down by the singing river
I find a strange delight
In murky pine-tree shadows
On a somber winter's night.
Though my feet turn toward the
  hilltop
When the moon is high,
I love the singing river
Under an inky sky.

REVELATION

The night was clear and cold and still.
You said, "I love you"—nothing more.
And in the silence following your words
I heard a hundred sounds not heard before.

The tinkling of a cowbell near the stream,
The bullfrog's husky croak, became part
Of a symphony of sound—an *obbligato*
For the drums within my heart.

PARTING

I saw you walk away with clouded eyes
And felt my heart grow heavy with despair,
For I am left with empty dreams, and care
Made darker by the sullen winter skies.
No longer shall we meet at close of day,
Stroll hand-in-hand along the bayou's edge;
To listen as the wind whips through the sedge
And watch the great blue heron stalk his prey.
Seeing the silver mullet cleave the air,
Hearing a bird-song muted by the breeze,
I stand alone beneath the moss-hung trees
But can I feel that you no longer care?
I could forgive your leaving did it not seem
That with you went my last and fondest dream.

THE LETTER

Strange that I remember
A little hill,
And trees,
The hollies and the pines.

You say
You love me still.
But I
Can read between the lines.

TREASURE

These things I treasure:
A slim new moon,
A fragmentary measure
Of an old familiar tune.
A cedar waxwing winging,
A flicker's sudden start
Can send a fountain springing
Upward in my heart.

STREETS OF CINTRA—PORTUGAL

Through the streets of Cintra
My heart is roaming still—
An earthen jug, a two-wheeled cart,
A vendor's piercing shrill;
Burros of the market-men
Saddled with their wares.
My eager feet go up and down
Cintra's street of stairs.

GARDEN NOTES

How strange to think a garden sown
For beauty of the eye alone
When many plants, their color flaunting,
Bear names so musical and haunting.
Like some old melody, but dear,
So falls *mimosa* on the ear;
And far-off chimes are faintly ringing
When *golden-bells* are swaying, swinging.
Laurel has loveliness of tone—
Gardens are not for eyes alone

MINSTRELSY

When the first sweet promise of morning
Stirs in the old pear tree,
My minstrel trills his gratitude
For the day that is yet to be.
He tilts on the topmost branches
As the sun begins to rise,
From there he flings his threads of praise
Into the red-gold skies.

PIETRO

Pietro sleeps at noonday:
Back to the olive tree, and chin on chest
Like some old man in retrospective mood.
The sun is warm, I know, I know,
But while you sleep, Pietro,
A breeze ripples the poppy bed; the ivy dances
Close to the crumbling wall. The very air
Is shot with arrows from the lake's blue gleaming.
Awake, Pietro! This is no time for dreaming.

NEW BROOMS

I bought new brooms today.
New brooms to sweep this New World dust
From age-old Kermanshahs,
And brighten Persian beauty
   into bloom.

REFLECTION

I thought of you as but an interlude
As one bright hour in a dull gray day,
And did not then foresee this bitter mood
That now bows down my heart with you away.
I had known love but as a simple thing,
A fancy that did easy come and go,
And no more lasting than a snow in spring.
How could I see that I should love you so?
Had I but thought when first I saw you smile,
That I should grow to love you more and more
And think of you with tears each little while
And with a heart more lonely than before—
Had I known then the things your smile implied
I might have turned before I reached your side.

A MEMORY

When I think back on childhood days
I do not see the town
But rather violets in the wood
And birches bending down,
The yellow jasmine that twines
The slash-pines on the hill,
And to my ear still faintly comes
A cardinal's merry trill.
When I look back I do not see
The busy streets of town,
But little pathways twisting through
The sedge grass, sere and brown.

MARCH WIND

There's a lovely song that the March wind sings,
A song of the joy that April brings—
A promise of leaves for bare brown trees,
A song of clover and bumble-bees,
And robins tilting on the eaves.

AWAKENING

Had I but lived some other shining spring,
Watched other clouds adrift in April skies,
I should remember blackbirds on the wing,
Not see them now reflected in your eyes.
I should remember live oaks near the shore
And bright azaleas flaming from afar,
Not see them through a partly-open door
That your dear hand but lately set ajar.
From other days of strolling in the sun
I should remember sailboats on the sound;
The small sandpipers as they dart and run
Are with me now. Such joy my heart has found!
Such loveliness it has been yours to give
That, loving you, I have begun to live.

SHADOWS

I remember April
That brought you to me
A sleek bird singing
In a pear tree;

And still another April
When our love was dead.
The pear tree sheltered
A mocking jay instead.

I am not afraid of winter
With dark and sullen skies.
But how can I face April
And look into her eyes?

IRIS

I can remember
Iris
Purple-petaled
In the sun,
A brick walk
Bordered
With iris,
One by one.

My blind eyes
Did not see them then.
But now
That love is done,
I can remember
Iris
Purple-petaled
In the sun.

REVERIE

I close my eyes. I do not see
The bustling city street
Nor hear the sounds of passing cars,
The shuffling, hurried feet—
But rather to my eye there comes
A scene that hurry quells—
Yellow butterflies that sway
Near Canterbury bells;
The hum of riveters becomes
A swarm of droning bees,
It seems I hear a cardinal's song,
And murmuring winds in trees.
The hurried, bustling city street
I never see at all—
But hollyhocks that primly stand
Along a whitewashed wall.

APRIL

Dark clouds spinning
Silver threads of rain
To wake the sleeping flowers
Upon the earth again.
Proud trees displaying
Green freshness of leaves,
Fat robins chirping,
Tilting on the eaves.

SNOW IN SPRING

There's snow in the old pear orchard
Though spring stirs in the breeze,
Though the grass is patched with clover
And the robins shrill quite over
The droning of the bees.
There's snow in the old pear orchard
On windy days like these—
The flakes are petals of blossoming pears
That sift through the boughs of the trees.

YESTERDAY

I found beauty yesterday
Along a lane of loveliness—
A larkspur's shining spire of blue
Glistened through the morning dew,
And bees droned songs of sweet content.

WIND SONG

The soft, warm wind of summer sings
Of eerie, half-fantastic things,
Of dragonflies with thin blue wings—
Of sunbeams sailing a lily boat
On a gleaming pool where broad leaves float
And a fish promenades in a Mandarin coat.
The warm sweet wind at morning sings
Of dragonflies with thin blue wings.

FORSYTHIA

Whenever I see forsythia
Bending with the breeze
I seem to hear the chiming notes
Of fairy melodies.
Titania must have danced, I think
To tinkling tunes like these.

BOAT SONG

White is the beach in the moonlight
And curved like a fluted shell,
My boat rides high on the crested waves
And rocks with the gentle swell;
The wind has a silken rustle
Like the swish of a trailing gown,
And strung like stars beyond the sands
Are the lights of the little town.

CHALLENGE

Here is a mountain
I must climb,
Straining step by step
With every fiber of my being.

And I care not to see
The other side
Now that youth and love
Are fleeing.

SOUTHERN GARDEN

Spring brings a wistful loveliness
To gardens of the South—
A faint perfume of jessamine,
And scarlet dragon's mouth.
A haunting pattern woven
On a magic loom.
(O sensitive mimosa
With mass of pink-tipped bloom!)
My heart still strolls in gardens
Though my feet may elsewhere stray.
(O Southern moon that shone upon
Acacia trees in May!)

TRUISM

Poems are found in simple things—
A blackbird's iridescent wings,
Swaying moss that swings from trees,
Murmuring music of the wind.
Beauty may the poet find
In simple things like these.

TETON SUNRISE

Jenny Lake at morning—
Its placid face
Ruffled by a passing breeze.

Birches—
Slender, white-barked,
Poised at the water's edge.

Mountains—
Majestic, silent,
Looking down on a sleepy cluster of tents.

The sun
A golden rim
Peering over the shoulder of a mountain.

PIETRO WRITES A SONNET

Pietro wrote a sonnet
One gleaming golden day.
His words danced on the paper
Like sailboats on the bay.

I begged him pause to hear my song
Or Francesca's new gavotte.
Pietro shook his curly head
And said he'd rather not.

I read Pietro's sonnet.
It was beyond compare!
The gold, the blue, the sea, the sky,
The music, all were there!

SONNET

I planned to love you but a little while,
A few short weeks—at most but half a year—
And then to take my leave, and let no tear
Mar the remembered sweetness of your smile.
I thought of you as but a simple child
(You seemed so innocent and sweet, my dear),
And since your eyes were candid, did not fear
That I, by you, should ever be beguiled.
Ah, but the charm of your simplicity
Has filled the emptiness that was my heart;
Your hands hold all of happiness for me—
(My dear, my dear if we should ever part!)
A little while I planned our love should last
But now I scheme of ways to hold it fast.

LITTLE BOATS OF JERBA

Oh, little boats of Jerba,
That skim across the bay
And match with sails of blue and gold
The gold and blue of day;
Why should I see you listing still
—When the sunset pales—
Oh, little boats of Jerba,
With blue and yellow sails?

AFTERTHOUGHT

Could I have stayed a little girl
With ribbons in my hair
I never could have loved you so
Nor known this blind despair;
It never could have torn my heart
To see you smiling there,
Had I but stayed a little girl
With ribbons in my hair.

REMEMBRANCE

The tender light that steals into your eyes,
Your sudden smile—remain
Between me and the somber winter skies.
I hear your voice above the rhapsody of rain.

JAPANESE FAN

It seemed like such a simple thing
To unfurl a paper fan—
But then I walked in gardens
In far-away Japan.

I strolled beside a sleeping stream
Where water lilies grew
And breathed the very air that came
From where magnolias blew.

The temple bells at Nikko
I heard with faint surprise,
And Fujiyama's snowy crest
Uprose before my eyes.

I stepped across a crescent bridge
And softly furled my fan—
For I had walked in gardens
In far-away Japan.

REVEALMENT

Although I wondered half the night
If your love were true,
I dreamed of him I loved before
I gave my heart to you.
And though I slept but fitfully,
At dawn, to my surprise,
I found myself so calm, so calm—
But oh, so old and wise.

SIMPLICITY

I hold things lovely
The simpler they are.
The phosphorescent flicker
Of a single silver star;
The fragile cobweb beauty
Of Queen Anne's lace.
Simplicity can hold so much
Of loveliness and grace!

TO A SECOND LOVE

I shall bear your love proudly
Like a banner
In the breeze. I shall bear your love
In such a manner
That those who see may think
My hurt heart healed,
Nor guess I bear your love before me
Like a shield.

GYPSY SONG

Many years ago, a gypsy queen died while camping near Meridian, Mississippi, and is buried there. When I was a small child, bands of gypsies made a pilgrimage to her grave each fall.

There are gypsy leaves on all the trees
And a gypsy wind in the air,
A whisper blew from over the hill—
A gypsy band is there.

Tonight the gypsies will build their fire
Near the grave of their father's queen,
And the wind will sing a gypsy song
And rattle his tambourine.

SPRING SONG

Come, go with me a-gypsying
When the long dreary winter is past,
Come, go with me a-gypsying
When springtime has come at last.
We'll wander carefree o'er hill and vale
We'll take no sorrows along,
Come, go with me a-gypsying,
Singing a joyful song.

Each night we'll camp away in the woods
By the side of some mirthful stream,
Over our heads the stars will shine,
And of the day's pleasures we'll dream.
Each morn we'll greet the rising sun,
Glad that the winter is past.
Come, go with me a-gypsying
For springtime has come at last.